# JOHN JACOBSON'S

## SUPER SONGS & SING-ALONGS
# U.S. PRESIDENTS

### NEW LYRICS TO OLD FAVORITES

## HAL•LEONARD®
### CORPORATION

7777 W. BLUEMOUND RD. P.O. BOX 13819 MILWAUKEE, WI 53213

Copyright © 2013 by HAL LEONARD CORPORATION
International Copyright Secured    All Rights Reserved

Visit Hal Leonard Online at
www.halleonard.com

# TABLE OF CONTENTS

# THE PRESIDENTS
## (OH, MY DARLING, CLEMENTINE)

Arranged with New Lyrics by JOHN JACOBSON
Piano Accompaniment by DEAN CROCKER

# OH, WHERE HAVE YOU BEEN, WASHINGTON?
## (BILLY BOY)

Arranged with New Lyrics by JOHN JACOBSON
Piano Accompaniment by DEAN CROCKER

# ADAMS, ADAMS
## (SAILING, SAILING)

Arranged with New Lyrics by JOHN JACOBSON
Piano Accompaniment by DEAN CROCKER

# HAIL, THOMAS JEFFERSON
## (HAIL, HAIL, THE GANG'S ALL HERE)

**Arranged with New Lyrics by JOHN JACOBSON**
**Piano Accompaniment by DEAN CROCKER**

Hail, Thom - as Jef - fer - son;

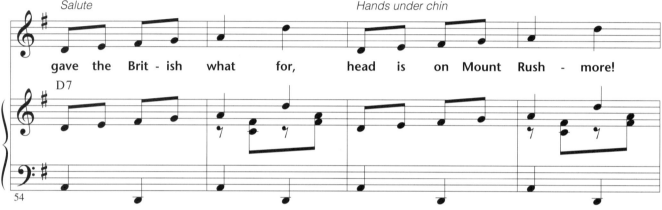

gave the Brit - ish what for, head is on Mount Rush - more!

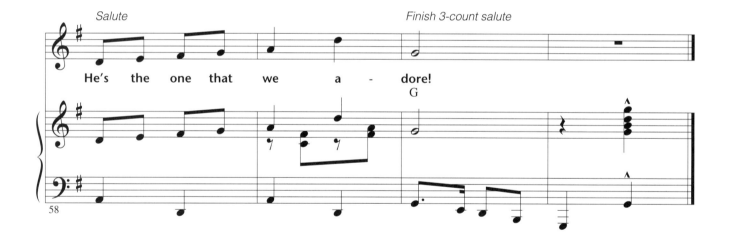

He's the one that we a - dore!

# FÜR LINCOLN
## (FÜR ELISE)

Arranged with New Lyrics by JOHN JACOBSON
Piano Accompaniment by DEAN CROCKER

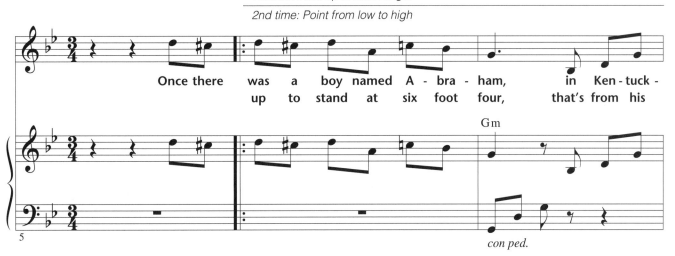

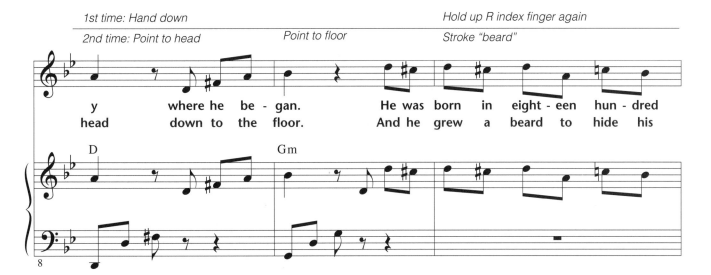

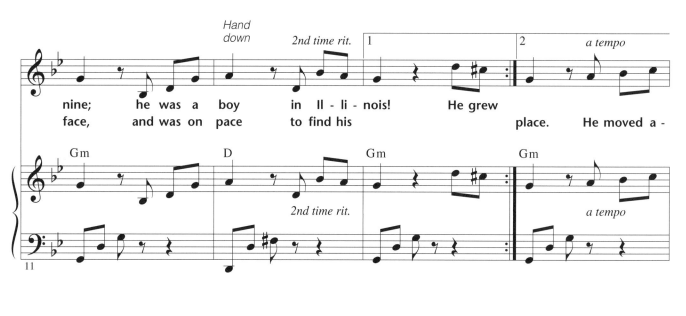

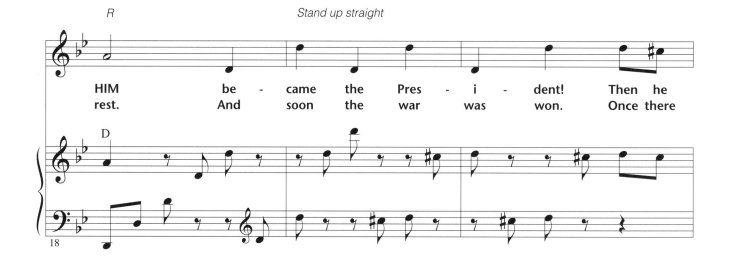

# CELEBRATE FDR
## (IT AIN'T GONNA RAIN NO MORE)

Arranged with New Lyrics by JOHN JACOBSON
Piano Accompaniment by DEAN CROCKER

# HIP HOORAY FOR JFK
## (YOU'RE A GRAND OLD FLAG)

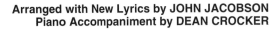
Arranged with New Lyrics by JOHN JACOBSON
Piano Accompaniment by DEAN CROCKER

**With thanks** (♩ = 132)

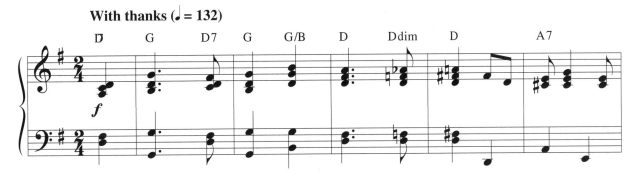

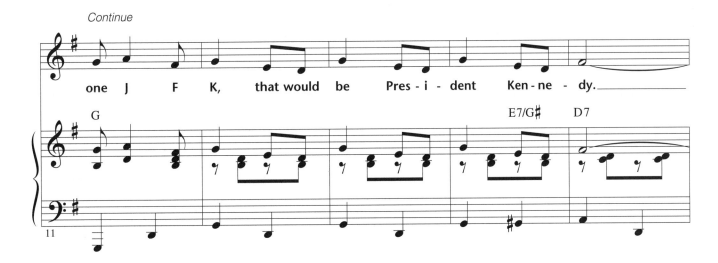

# LOOK, RONALD REAGAN
## (WAIT FOR THE WAGON)

Arranged with New Lyrics by JOHN JACOBSON
Piano Accompaniment by DEAN CROCKER

*Hook thumbs in belt loops*

There
He
One

*With feet apart, rock hips from side to side*

L  R  L  R  L  R  Plié

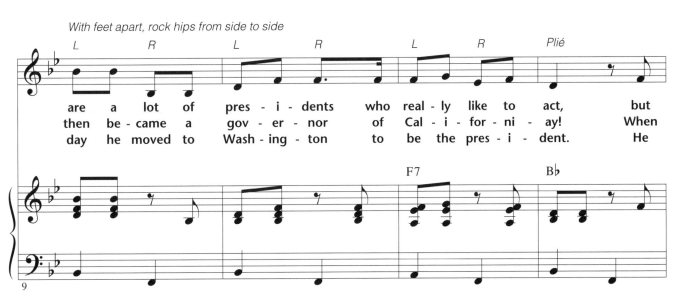

are a lot of pres - i - dents who real - ly like to act, but
then be - came a gov - er - nor of Cal - i - for - ni - ay! When
day he moved to Wash - ing - ton to be the pres - i - dent. He

# OBAMA
## (BINGO)

Arranged with New Lyrics by JOHN JACOBSON
Piano Accompaniment by DEAN CROCKER

# PARTY WITH THE PRESIDENTS
## (LA DONNA È MOBILE)

Arranged with New Lyrics by JOHN JACOBSON
Piano Accompaniment by DEAN CROCKER

Simply (♩ = 144)

*Clap hands at head level, off to the L on beats 2 and 3 of each measure*

*Clap on 2 and 3, switching sides on each measure*

Let's have some fun to-day,
We're mad for Mad-i-son,

the An-dy Jack-son way, and oth-er res-i-dents
our fill of Fill-more, too, and for some ex-tra fun,

# JOHN JACOBSON'S

## SUPER SONGS & SING-ALONGS
# U.S. PRESIDENTS

# REPRODUCIBLE LYRIC PAGES

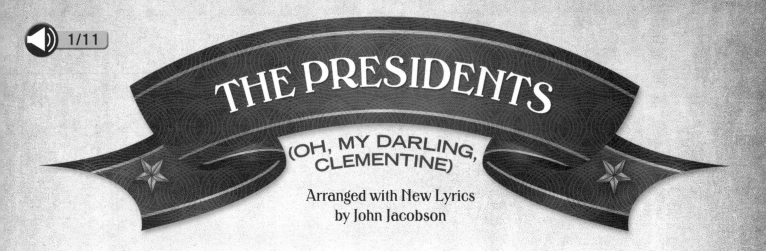

# THE PRESIDENTS

## (OH, MY DARLING, CLEMENTINE)

Arranged with New Lyrics
by John Jacobson

If you want to name the presidents,
start with George Washington!
Add John Adams, Thomas Jefferson,
Madison and James Monroe.

John Quincy Adams, Andrew Jackson,
and Martin Van Buren, too.
William Harrison and John Tyler,
James K. Polk, to name a few.

Zachary Taylor, Millard Filmore,
Franklin Pierce, and Buchanan, too.
Then there's Lincoln, Andrew Johnson,
U.S. Grant and R.B. Hayes.

Garfield and Arthur, Grover Cleveland,
Harrison, so nice and svelt.
Grover once more, Bill McKinley,
then there's Teddy Roosevelt!

William Taft, Wilson, Harding,
Coolidge, Hoover, F D R,
Harry Truman, Eisenhower,
John F. Kennedy, L B J!

Richard Nixon, Gerald Ford,
Jimmy Carter, Reagan, Yah!
George the 1st Bush, William Clinton,
George W. Bush, Obama!

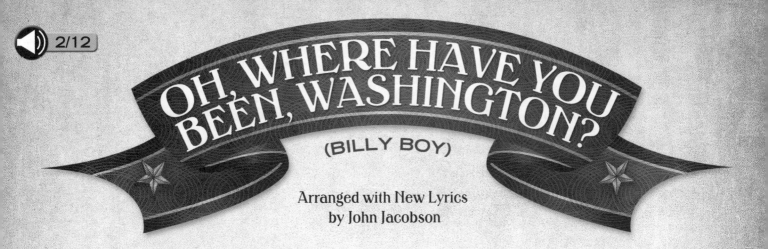

# OH, WHERE HAVE YOU BEEN, WASHINGTON?

## (BILLY BOY)

Arranged with New Lyrics
by John Jacobson

Oh, where have you been, Washington, Washington?
Oh, where have you been, Mister President?
"Oh, I'd like to tell you more, but I'm headed for a war!"
You're a keeper and Father of our country.

Will you cross the Delaware, Washington, Washington?
Will you cross the Delaware, Mister President?
"Yes, I'll cross the Delaware! I'm the only one to dare!"
You're a keeper and Father of our country.

Did you chop that cherry tree, Washington, Washington?
Did you chop that cherry tree, Mister President?
"Oh, I can not tell a lie, so I tell you it was I!"
You're a keeper and Father of our country.

Are you wearing wooden teeth, Washington, Washington?
Are you wearing wooden teeth, Mister President?
"Yes, I'm wearing wooden teeth, but my gums are underneath!"
You're a keeper and Father of our country.

Can you sit astride a horse, Washington, Washington?
Can you sit astride a horse, Mister President?
"I can sit astride a horse; astride a horse, I sit of course!"
You're a keeper and Father of our country.

Do you like your monument, Washington, Washington?
Do you like your monument, Mister President?
"Sure I like my monument. It's worth every cent you spent!"
You're a keeper and Father of our country.

OK TO
REPRODUCE

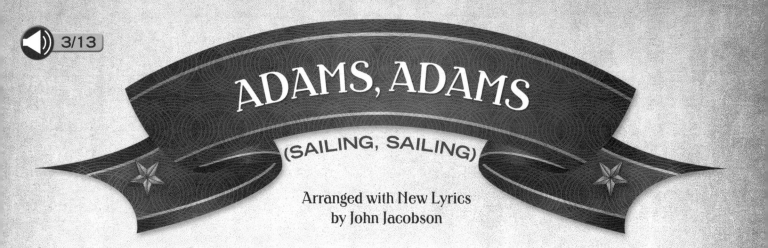

# ADAMS, ADAMS

## (SAILING, SAILING)

Arranged with New Lyrics
by John Jacobson

Young John Adams started off rather slow!
Then he met Abigail and his luck began to grow!
Adams, Adams worked for George Washington.
He was the first Vice President when our Nation had begun!

Young John Adams, our second president,
came out of Massachusetts with the noblest of intent!
Adams, Adams ran again, but didn't win.
Although he fought the noble fight, he lost to Jefferson!

Adams, Adams had a son by the name of John.
He was our sixth president and he moved to Washington!
Old John Adams finally passed away,
the same day as Thomas Jefferson, on Independence Day!

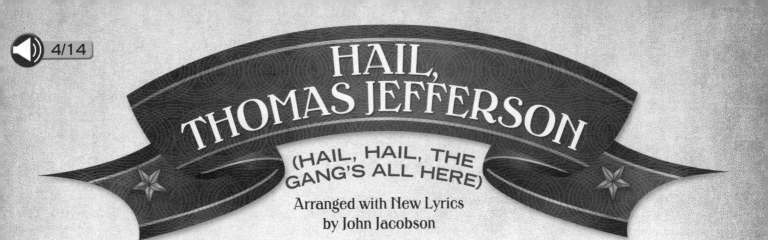

# HAIL, THOMAS JEFFERSON

## (HAIL, HAIL, THE GANG'S ALL HERE)

Arranged with New Lyrics
by John Jacobson

Hail, Thomas Jefferson;
Laid a good foundation, wrote the Declaration.
Hail, Thomas Jefferson,
President number three!

Hail, Thomas Jefferson;
Lived at Monticello, played a little cello!
Hail, Thomas Jefferson;
President number three!

*(chanted)*
Washington was number one!
Adams was number two!
Next came Thomas Jefferson!
We like Thomas Jefferson!
Spent a lot of time in France!
We would like to go to France!
Even learned a little dance!
Hoo-ray!

*(sing)*
Hail, Thomas Jefferson;
Liked to play piana, purchased Louisiana!
Hail, Thomas Jefferson;
Gave the British what for,
Head is on Mount Rushmore!
He's the one that we adore!

# FÜR LINCOLN

## (FÜR ELISE)

**Arranged with New Lyrics
by John Jacobson**

Once there was a boy named Abraham,
In Kentucky where he began.
He was born in eighteen hundred nine;
He was a boy in Illinois!

He grew up to stand at six foot four,
That's from his head down to the floor.
And he grew a beard to hide his face,
And was on pace to find his place.

He moved around, but soon he found a place for him.
For AbraHIM became the President!

Then he had to run the Civil War;
It was a chore he didn't ask for.
And he had to end all slavery;
Some thought him nuts, but he had guts!

Oh, Honest Abe, he did his best and didn't whine,
He didn't rest, and soon the war was won.

Once there was a man named Abraham
Who pulled us through; his word was true.
So we give it up to Abraham,
That's President Lincoln to you!

# CELEBRATE FDR

## (IT AIN'T GONNA RAIN NO MORE)

Arranged with New Lyrics
by John Jacobson

Let's celebrate ol' FDR,
Our president for twelve years.
Chatting 'round the fireplace,
He told us all to have no fears!

Let's celebrate ol' FDR,
And his wife Eleanor.
She did much with her soft touch,
And helped to save the sick and poor.

Good ol' Franklin,
Dealt with the Depression.
So…

Let's celebrate ol' FDR,
He had broad appeal.
And when things were really rough,
He gave us all a brand New Deal!

How can we thank the president
Who served the most by far?
Let's give a cheer and have no fear
And celebrate ol' FDR!

# HIP HOORAY FOR JFK

## (YOU'RE A GRAND OLD FLAG)

Arranged with New Lyrics
by John Jacobson

Give a hip hooray for the one JFK,
That would be President Kennedy.
He came on the scene in nineteen seventeen
And became president thirty-five!

Back in World War II, he had plenty to do,
When his boat got so sunk at sea *(at sea)* !
We're telling you, he saved his crew,
And we all went on to victory!

"K" is for the kindness that he offered.
"E" is everything he battled for.
Double "N" is never, never be a downer.
"E" is for the energy he bore.
"D" is for his dashing, daring nature.
"Y" is for the youth he gave the day.
Put them all together, they spell **Kennedy**!
It's shorter to say JFK!

Give a hip hooray for the one JFK,
That would be President Kennedy.
And to help him win, he married Jacqueline.
They were both oh, so good and so wise.

Yes, he fought and taught and he made Camelot,
And he worked so hard every day!
Oh John Fitzgerald Kennedy,
Let's all give a cheer for JFK! *Hooray!*

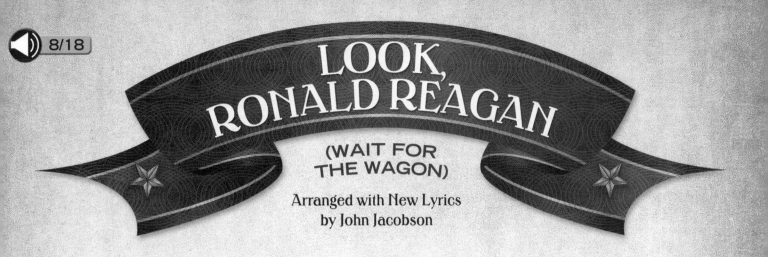

# LOOK, RONALD REAGAN
## (WAIT FOR THE WAGON)

Arranged with New Lyrics
by John Jacobson

There are a lot of presidents who really like to act,
But one was first an actor, that's a presidential fact!
Look, Ronald Reagan! Look, Ronald Reagan!
Look, Ronald Reagan, you're a real movie star!

He then became a governor of Californi-ay!
When he was spotted on the street, someone would always say,
Look, Ronald Reagan! Look, Ronald Reagan!
Look, Ronald Reagan, you're a real movie star!

One day he moved to Washington to be the president.
He moved into the White House, didn't have to pay the rent!
Look, Ronald Reagan! Look, Ronald Reagan!
Look, Ronald Reagan, you're a real movie star!

Oh, he was number forty, he graced the silver screen.
He liked to ride his pony and he loved his jelly beans.
Look, Ronald Reagan! Look, Ronald Reagan!
Look, Ronald Reagan, you're a movie star!
And you came so far!
We like Nancy, too!
We give thanks to you!

# OBAMA

## (BINGO)

Arranged with New Lyrics
by John Jacobson

A president from Illinois,
Obama was his name!
O-B-A-M-A, O-B-A-M-A, O-B-A-M-A,
Obama was his name.

Born in nineteen sixty-one,
He grew up in Hawaii.
(x) B-A-M-A, (x) B-A-M-A, (x) B-A-M-A,
Obama was his name.

He went to University,
And soon became a lawyer!
(x x) A-M-A, (x x) A-M-A, (x x) A-M-A,
Obama was his name.

He married a fine lady,
Who liked the name Obama!
(x x x) M-A, (x x x) M-A, (x x x) M-A,
Obama was his name.

He then became a senator,
And wrote some weighty books!
(x x x x) A, (x x x x) A, (x x x x) A,
Obama was his name.

The forty-fourth president
of the United States,
(x x x x x), (x x x x x), (x x x x x)
Obama was his name!

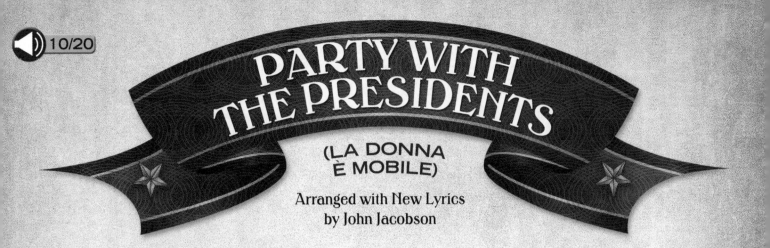

# PARTY WITH THE PRESIDENTS
## (LA DONNA È MOBILE)

Arranged with New Lyrics
by John Jacobson

Let's have some fun today,
The Andy Jackson way,
And other residents,
Who were our presidents!

We'll play with FDR!
Coolidge will take us far!
Let's have a holiday,
The Herbert Hoover way!

Look at Zachary Taylor
Tag along with Tyler!
Even Eisenhower
Is ready to have some fun!

JFK, LBJ,
Bring on Benjamin Harrison.
Gerald Ford, Howard Taft,
Even George Washington!

We're mad for Madison,
Our fill of Fillmore, too,
And for some extra fun,
There's Thomas Jefferson.

Who's heard of Franklin Pierce?
We heard his glare was fierce.
And since we're on the go,
Let's bring on James Monroe.

When the party's sinkin',
Bring on old Abe Lincoln!
Everyone agrees,
Harry Truman is a blast!

JFK, LBJ,
Oh, and here we go again.
Rutherford, Theodore,
And Martin Van Buren!

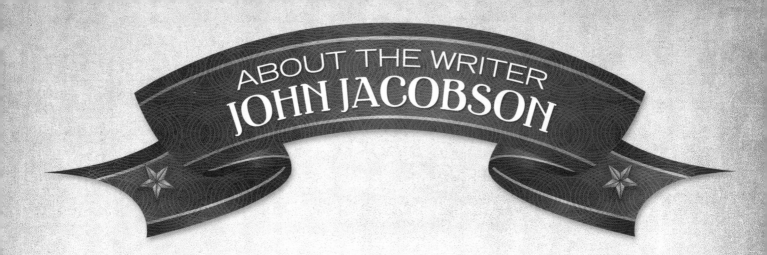

# ABOUT THE WRITER
# JOHN JACOBSON

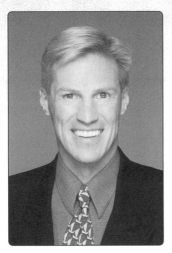

In October of 2001 President George Bush named John Jacobson a *Point of Light* award winner for his "dedication to providing young people involved in the arts opportunities to combine music, charitable giving and community service." John is the founder and volunteer president of *America Sings!* Inc., a non-profit organization that encourages young performers to use their time and talents for community service. With a bachelor's degree in Music Education from the University of Wisconsin-Madison and a Master's Degree in Liberal Studies from Georgetown University, John is recognized internationally as a creative and motivating speaker for teachers and students involved in choral music education. He is the author and composer of many musicals and choral works that have been performed by millions of children worldwide, as well as educational videos and tapes that have helped music educators excel in their individual teaching arenas, all published exclusively by Hal Leonard Corporation. John has staged hundreds of huge music festival ensembles in his association with Walt Disney Productions and directed productions featuring thousands of young singers including NBC's national broadcast of the Macy's Thanksgiving Day Parade, presidential inaugurations and more. John stars in children's musical and exercise videotapes, including the series *Jjump!* A Fitness Program for Children and is the Senior Contributing Writer for *John Jacobson's Music Express*, an educational magazine for young children published by Hal Leonard Corporation. Most recently, John has become a YouTube sensation and is known by millions as the "Double Dream Hands Guy!"